WHY RELATIONSHIP FIRST WORKS

Why and How It Changes Everything

All photos by Kathleen Camp

Published in the United States by 14 Hands Press,

an imprint of Camp Horse Camp, LLC

www.14handspress.com

Some of the material herein has appeared

in other books by Joe Camp

Library of Congress subject headings

Camp, Joe

Why Relationship First Works / by Joe Camp

Horses

Human-animal relationships

Horses-health

Horsemanship

The Soul of a Horse: Life Lessons from the Herd

ISBN 978-1-930681-43-9

First Edition

WHY RELATIONSHIP FIRST WORKS

Why and How It Changes Everything

JOE CAMP

14 HANDS PRESS

"Joe Camp is a master storyteller." - *THE NEW YORK TIMES*

"Joe Camp is a natural when it comes to understanding how animals tick and a genius at telling us their story. His books are must-reads for those who love animals of any species." - *MONTY ROBERTS, AUTHOR OF NEW YORK TIMES BEST-SELLER THE MAN WHO LISTENS TO HORSES*

"Camp has become something of a master at telling us what can be learned from animals, in this case specifically horses, without making us realize we have been educated, and, that is, perhaps, the mark of a real teacher. The tightly written, simply designed, and powerfully drawn chapters often read like short stories that flow from the heart." - *JACK L. KENNEDY, THE JOPLIN INDEPENDENT*

"One cannot help but be touched by Camp's love and sympathy for animals and by his eloquence on the subject." - *MICHAEL KORDA, THE WASHINGTON POST*

"Joe Camp is a gifted storyteller and the results are magical. Joe entertains, educates and empowers, baring his own soul while articulating keystone principles of a modern revolution in horsemanship." - *RICK LAMB, AUTHOR AND TV/RADIO HOST "THE HORSE SHOW"*

Visit The Soul of a Horse Channel on Vimeo or
YouTube to watch the Video of Joe and Cash:
Relationship First!

For Kathleen, who loved me enough to initiate all this when she was secretly terrified of horses

CONTENTS

INTRODUCTION

Often, in the early evening, when the stresses of the day are weighing heavy, I pack it in and head out to the pasture. I'll sit on my favorite rock, or just stand, with my shoulders slumped, head down, and wait. It's never long before I feel the magical tickle of whiskers against my neck, or the elixir of warm breath across my ear, a restoring rub against my cheek. I have spoken their language and they have responded. And my problems have vanished. This book is written for everyone who has never experienced this miracle.

- Joe Camp
The Soul of a Horse
Life Lessons from the Herd

1

IN THE BEGINNING

I remember that it was an unusually chilly day for late May, because I recall the jacket I was wearing. Not so much the jacket, I suppose, as the collar. The hairs on the back of my neck were standing at full attention, and the collar was scratching at them.

There was no one else around. Just me and this eleven-hundred pound creature I had only met once before. And today he was passing out no clues as to how he felt about that earlier meeting, or about me. His stare was without emotion. Empty. Scary to one who was taking his very first step into the world of horses.

If he chose to do so this beast could take me out with no effort whatsoever. He was less than fifteen feet away. No halter, no line. We were surrounded by a round pen a mere fifty feet in diameter. No place to hide. Not that he was mean. At least I had been told that he wasn't. But I had also been told that anything is possible with a horse. He's a prey animal, they had said. A freaky flight animal that can flip from quiet and thoughtful to wild and reactive in a single heartbeat. Accidents happen.

I knew very little about this horse, and none of it firsthand. Logic said do not depend upon hearsay. Be sure. There's nothing like firsthand knowledge. But all I knew was what I could see. He was big.

The sales slip stated that he was unregistered. And his name was Cash.

But there was something about him. A kindness in his eyes that betrayed the vacant expression. And sometimes he would cock his head as if he were asking a question. I wanted him to be more than chattel. I wanted a relationship with this horse. I wanted to begin at the beginning, as Monty Roberts had prescribed. *Start with a blank sheet of paper, then fill it in.*

Together.

I'm not a gambler. Certainty is my mantra. Knowledge over luck. But on this day I was gambling.

I had never done this before.

I knew dogs.

I did not know horses.

And I was going to ask this one to do something he had probably never been asked to do in his lifetime. To make a choice. Which made me all the more nervous. What if it didn't work?

What if his choice was not *me*?

I was in that round pen because a few weeks earlier my wife, Kathleen, had pushed me out of bed one morning and instructed me to get dressed and get in the car.

"Where are we going?" I asked several times.

"You'll see."

Being the paranoid, suspicious type, whenever my birthday gets close, the ears go up and twist in the wind.

The brain shuffled and dealt. Nothing came up.

We drove down the hill and soon Kathleen was whipping in at a sign for the local animal shelter.

Another dog? I wondered. We have four. Four's enough.

She drove right past the next turn for the animal shelter and pulled into a park. There were a few picnic tables scattered about. And a big horse trailer.

The car jerked to a stop and Kathleen looked at me and smiled. "Happy birthday," she said.

"What?" I said. "What??"

"You said we should go for a trail ride sometime." She grinned. "*Sometime* is today."

Two weeks later we owned three horses.

We should've named them Impulsive, Compulsive, and Obsessive.

Our house was way out in the country and it came with a couple of horse stalls, both painted a crisp white, one of them covered with a rusty red roof. They were cute. Often, over the three years we had lived there, we could be found in the late afternoon sitting on our front porch, looking out over the stalls, watching the sun sink beneath the ridge of mountains to the west. One of us would say "Those stalls surely seem empty." Or, "Wouldn't it be nice if there were a couple of horses ambling back and forth down in the stalls?"

Like a postcard.

A lovely picture at sunset.

With cute horse stalls.

Lesson #1: Cute horse stalls are not adequate reason to purchase three horses.

Never mind the six we own now.

We had no idea what we were getting into. Thank God for a chance meeting with Monty Roberts. Well, not a *real* meeting. We were making the obligatory trip that new horse owners must make to Boot Barn when Kathleen picked up a *California Horse Trader*. As we sat around a table watching the kids chomp cheese burgers, she read an article about Monty and passed it over to me. That's how I came to find myself in a round pen that day staring off our big new Arabian.

Monty is an amazing man, with an incredible story. His book *The Man Who Listens to Horses* has sold something like five and a half million copies and was on the *New York Times* best-seller list for 58 weeks! I ordered his book and a DVD of one of his *Join-Up* demonstrations the minute I got home, and was completely blown away. In the video, he took a horse that had never had as much as a halter on him, never mind a saddle or rider, and in thirty minutes caused that horse to *choose* to be with him, to accept a saddle, and a rider, all with no violence, pain, or even stress to the horse!

Thirty minutes!

It takes "traditional" horse trainers weeks to get to that point, the ones who still tie horses legs together and crash them to the ground, then spend days upon days scaring the devil out of them, proving to the horse that humans are, in fact, the predators he's always thought we were. They usually get there, these traditional trainers, but it's by force, and submission, and fear. Not trust, or respect.

Or choice.

In retrospect, for me, the overwhelming key to what I saw Monty do in thirty minutes, is the fact that the horse made the decision, the choice. The horse chose Monty as a herd member and leader. And from that point on, everything was built on trust, not coercion. And what a difference that makes.

And it was simple.

Not rocket science.

I watched the DVD twice and was off to the round pen.

It changed my life forever.

This man is responsible for us beginning our relationship with horses as it *should* begin, and propelling us onto a journey of discovery into a truly enigmatic world. A world that has reminded me that you cannot, in fact, tell a book by its cover; that no "expert" should

ever be beyond question just because somebody somewhere has given him or her such a label. That every-
body and everything is up for study. That logic and
good sense still provide the most reasonable answers,
and still, given exposure, will prevail.

It's a mystery to me how people can ignore what
seems so obvious, so logical, simply because it would
mean *change*. Even though the change is for the better.
I say look forward to the opportunity to learn something new. Relish and devour knowledge with gusto.
Always be reaching for the best possible way to do
things. It keeps you alive, and healthy, and happy. And
makes for a better world.

Just because something has *always been done* a certain way does not necessarily mean it's the best way, or
the correct way, or the healthiest way for your horse, or
your relationship with your horse, or your life. Especially if, after asking a few questions, the traditional way
defies logic and good sense, and falls short on compassion and respect.

The truth is too many horse owners are shortening
their horses' lives, degrading their health, and limiting
their happiness by the way they keep and care for them.
But it doesn't have to be that way. Information is king.
Gather it from every source, make comparisons, and
evaluate results. And don't take just one opinion as gos-
pel. Not mine or anyone else's. Soon you'll not only feel

better about what you're doing, you'll do it better. And the journey will be fascinating.

We were only a year and a half into this voyage with horses as these words found their way into the computer, but it was an obsessive, compulsive year and a half, and the wonderful thing about being a newcomer is that you start with a clean plate. No baggage. No preconceptions. No musts. Just a desire to learn what's best for our horses, and our relationship with them. And a determination to use logic and knowledge wherever found, even if it means exposing a few myths about what does, in fact, produce the best results.

Cash was pawing the ground now, wondering, I suspect, why I was just standing there in the round pen doing nothing. The truth is I was reluctant to start the process. Nervous. Rejection is not one of my favorite concepts. Once started, I would soon be asking him to make his choice. What if he said no? Is that it? Is it over? Does he go back to his previous owner?

I have often felt vulnerable during my sixty-eight years, but rarely *this* vulnerable. I really *wanted* this horse to choose me.

What if I screw it up? Maybe I won't do it right. It's my first time. What if he runs over me? Actually, that was the lowest on my list of concerns because Monty's Join-Up process is built on the language of the horse, and the fact that the raw horse inherently perceives humans as predators. Their response is flight, not fight. It's as automatic as breathing.

Bite the bullet, Joe, I kept telling myself. Give him the choice.

I had vowed that this would be our path. We would begin our relationship with every horse in this manner. Our way to true horsemanship, which, as I would come to understand, was not about how well you ride, or how many trophies you win, or how fast your horse runs, or how high he or she jumps.

I squared my shoulders, stood tall, looked this almost sixteen hands of horse straight in the eye, appearing as much like a predator as I could muster, and tossed one end of a soft long-line into the air behind him, and off he went at full gallop around the round pen. Just like Monty said he would.

Flight.

I kept my eyes on his eyes, just as a predator would. Cash would run for roughly a quarter of a mile, just as horses do in the wild, before he would offer his first signal. Did he actually think I was a predator, or did he know he was being tested? I believe it's somewhere in between, a sort of leveling of the playing field. A starting from scratch with something he knows ever so well. Predators and flight. A simulation, if you will. Certainly he was into it. His eyes were wide, his nostrils flared. At the very least he wasn't sure about me, and those fifty-five million years of genetics were telling him to flee.

It was those same genetics that caused him to offer the first signal. His inside ear turned and locked on me, again as Monty had predicted. He had run the quarter of a mile that usually preserves him from most predators; and I was still there, but not really seeming very predatory. So now, instead of pure reactive flight, he was getting curious. Beginning to *think* about it. Maybe he was even a bit confused. Horses have two nearly separate brains. Some say one is the reactive brain and the other is the thinking brain. Whether or not that's true physiologically, emotionally it's a good analogy. When they're operating from the reactive side, the rule of thumb is to stand clear until you can get them thinking. Cash was now shifting. He was beginning to think. *Hmm, maybe this human is not a predator after all. I'll just keep an ear out for a bit. See what happens.*

Meanwhile, my eyes were still on his eyes, my shoulders square, and I was still tossing the line behind him.

Before long, he began to lick and chew. Signal number two. *I think maybe it's safe to relax. I think, just maybe, this guy's okay. I mean, if he really wanted to hurt me, he's had plenty of time, right?*

And, of course, he was right. But, still, I kept up the pressure. Kept him running. Waiting for the next signal.

It came quickly. He lowered his head, almost to the ground, and began to narrow the circle. Signal number three. *I'll look submissive, try to get closer, see what happens. I think this guy might be a good leader. We should discuss it.*

He was still loping, but slower now. Definitely wanting to negotiate. That's when I was supposed to take my eyes off him, turn away, and lower my head and shoulders. No longer predatorial, but assuming a submissive stance of my own, saying *Okay, if it's your desire, come on in. I'm not going to hurt you. But the choice is yours.*

The moment of truth. Would he in fact do that? Would he make the decision, totally on his own, to come to me? I took a deep breath, and turned away.

He came to a halt and stood somewhere behind me.

The seconds seemed like hours.

"Don't look back," Monty had warned. "Just stare at the ground."

A tiny spider was crawling across my new Boot Barn boot. The collar of my jacket was tickling the hairs on the back of my neck. And my heart was pounding. Then a puff of warm, moist air brushed my ear. My heart skipped a beat. He was really close. Then I felt his nose on my shoulder... the moment of *Join-Up*. I couldn't believe it. Tears came out of nowhere and streamed down my cheeks. I had spoken to him in his language, and he had listened... and he had chosen to be with me. His choice. Of his own free will he had said *I trust you.* And that's when everything changed. Because without that choice, his choice, there is no relationship. Without his choice, he is only a prisoner.

I turned and rubbed him on the face, then walked off across the pen. Cash followed, right off my shoulder, wherever I went.

Such a rush I haven't often felt.

I was no longer a horse *owner.* I was a companion. A leader. A trusted friend. A big brother. And I promised him that his life with me would be the very best that I could possibly make it.

I had no clue what the very best might be but I vowed to him I would find out.

And what a difference it has made as this newcomer has stumbled his way through the learning process. Cash has never stopped trying, never stopped listening, never stopped giving.

Nor have I.

The above is an edited excerpt from the best selling book The Soul of a Horse – Life Lessons from the Herd by Joe Camp.

2

WHY RELATIONSHIP?

Why are we still where we are today, with so many owners of horses missing the very best part of horse ownership? The reason, I believe, is that most people do not begin at the beginning. They want to start halfway around the track, instead of in the starting gate.

I now have a horse. I want to do something with it. Go riding. Compete. Something!

We humans are in such a hurry that there's no time to allow for trust, which is necessary for any relationship. To learn to communicate. To gain and give trust and understanding. To walk in the horse's boots, so to speak.

To begin at the beginning.

The beginning for us was building relationship through our discovery of Monty Roberts and his Join-Up process.

Why?

I ask that question a lot.

To a fault.

Kathleen says it often seems that *why* is the only word I know.

Whyyyy?

So, *why* do I feel so strongly about Monty Roberts' Join-Up?

Because it answers the *why* questions right up front:

Why does it work?

Because it speaks to the horse's genetics in the horse's own language, the language of the herd. Which is all built upon the fact that the horse is a prey animal, a flight animal. And safety and security are his number one concerns, at the top of his forever wish list. The horse would always rather be in a safe and secure relationship than not.

Why do you say anyone can do it?

Because it's simple. Easy to accomplish. Straight to the point, using a very specific "1-2-3" kind of "to-do" list that anyone can understand and handle. I managed to accomplish Join-Up after watching Monty's DVD only twice (previous chapter).

Why does it cause the horse to – as you say – change forever?

Because the horse does the joining-up of his own free will. He chooses you, not vice-versa. It's his choice whether or not to say to you *I trust you to be my leader.* If you in any way coerce the horse into being close to you, into accepting you or your training, if you force yourself or your will on the horse there will be no change in the horse. The willingness, the "try" will not be there.

But... once trust has been earned of the horse's free choice, then you must be a good leader. That becomes the number one goal.

The determining factor of who *leads* who in the herd is who *moves* who. That means ground work on your part, and a good bit of it. And this is where a lot of folks get into trouble and don't understand the outcome.

Many like to think that once Joined-Up, once the horse has said *I trust you*, the horse is going to be like a smoochie puppy. It's all going to be cuddles and hugs and kisses. But a horse is not a smoochie puppy, not even close. The horse's idea of a good relationship, first and foremost, is a feeling of safety. The security of knowing he is being lead by a good leader who will keep him safe. The horse doesn't fall in love with the horse above him in the herd, or out of love with the one below him. And this is difficult for most humans to grasp. Humans want relationship to be an emotional thing, but it simply isn't in the life and language of the herd. At least not to the extent as it is with humans, or even dogs. Yes, they can like being with you, but mostly it's about safety and security.

Not to say that once the horse's security, his trust, is well in place there won't be a bond. There will be. Very much so. It'll just be different than what most humans perceive as a bond. There could even be a shared hug or kiss here and there with some horses, but not necessarily with all horses. It depends upon the personality of the horse. We have eight and they're all different. Some show moments of affection, some not so much. But the bond and relationship is strong with all of them.

And because their trust came of their own free choice they all give back, try harder, and are more willing. Truly. When that moment came everything changed.

What your relationship turns into after you have their trust depends upon you and how good a leader your are. In other words, how well and how easily you can move the horse's every-body-part whenever and wherever you want. Another concept that is sometimes hard for humans to grasp: the simple idea that who moves who can determine leadership, bolster relationship, and select one's place in the herd.

Is Monty's Join-Up in a round pen the only way to begin a relationship with your horse?

No, of course not. There are more ways to Join Up than one can count.

Our Mouse had not been exposed to the round pen join-up when she made her choice to Join Up. It all happened with Monty in a "square pen". When she left Iowa to travel to Monty's California ranch it took six men to get Mouse into a trailer. It took Monty ten minutes to convince her, using her language, to come to him and say *I trust you to be my leader*. A moment later Monty was addressing his group of students using Mouse's back as a podium to lean on. Just amazing.

Saffron, our new mustang who came to us pregnant, from the wild via one of the BLM's illegal mustang roundups, took 35 evenings of what we call *No Agenda Time* to make her choice. It was on the evening of my birthday as Kathleen and I sat in her paddock chatting about the day. For the 35 days since she arrived I had not been able to touch her. At all. I couldn't even stand up if she was nearby without her bolting for the other end of the paddock. But on that evening, as if a switch was thrown, she went from zero to a hundred in an instant. See our blog post: An Amazing Birthday Gift from a Wild Mustang.

Saffron made her choice on my birthday

She was suddenly all over me, and I could rub her anywhere I chose, including her ears and feet. She had cleaned her plate of any past human experiences with the BLM and was now saying, completely and fully, *I trust you.*

But every version of Join Up that truly works depends upon the same two key ingredients that must be present or the relationship will never be what it should be, what it could be.

It must be the horse's choice to trust you or not, to be in relationship with you, or not. And you must continue prove to the horse that you are his leader, a *good* leader. In *his* language (see <u>Beginning Ground Work</u>). Those are the two secret ingredients. And no one else, in my experience, has ever made it as clear or as simple as Monty Roberts.

Pat and Linda Parelli have their own way of accomplishing the same end relationship with their horses, which definitely includes giving the horse the choice to trust and be in relationship. They just don't call it join-up and it's not as simple or as "1-2-3" as Monty's Join-Up. Or as lazy and easy our <u>No Agenda Time</u>.

Another thing about Join-Up that I find to be very cool is that very recently The International Society of Equitation Science published a scientific study comparing Monty's Join-Up to a conventional training method used in the United Kingdom and found that the heart rates observed from Monty Roberts trained horses during first saddle and first rider were not only significantly lower than the conventional method, they were the lowest reported for any training regime reported in the literature to date. Further reporting that the technique of Join-up has been frequently criticized and reported in

the literature to be a significant stressor due to the per-
ceived opinion that this method overtly activates the
flight response, the study could find no evidence that
the use of the round pen or, indeed the technique of
Join-up, was fear inducing and thus a significant stress-
or to the horse based on heart rate alone. "In fact, we
found that the heart rate of horses during this technique
were considerably below the maximum heart rate for
horses of this age and breed."

Still further, after 20 days of training (30
minutes/horse/day) the study horses undertook a stand-
ardized ridden obstacle and flatwork test and a ridden
freestyle test. Monty's trained horses scored significantly higher in all three tests as determined by a panel of
judges who were unaware of the study or the trainers
involved in the study.

3

MARIAH

Leaning on the fence next to me, elbows propped on the top rail, was a true cowboy. Gnarled and weathered, crusty as they come, and a likable sort. Full of tales and experiences. He must've been near my age and had been riding since he was old enough to hold on. I actually paused long enough to absorb the moment, me with my Boot Barn boots and new straw hat, right there in the thick of it. Me and him. Cowboys.

Then he spoke for only the third time since Mariah had come out of her stall, and the reverence I was feeling cracked and shattered like the coyote in a Roadrunner cartoon.

Mariah was a cute little Arabian mare that the cowboy had for sale. Kathleen and I were still looking for the right horse for her. The cowboy had watched me earlier in Mariah's stall, just hanging out, waiting for her to tell me it was okay to put on the halter. She never did. The cowboy had asked, "Do you want me to catch her?"

It made me uneasy, but I said, "No thanks." It was that thing about choice again. Trying not to seem so much like a predator by racing into the stall and slapping the halter on first thing, horse willing or not. But I couldn't push away the feeling of embarrassment. Even incompetence. As if I were being challenged. I knew I could corner her and catch her. The stall wasn't that big. But I was attempting to stir some sort of relationship. Not my will over hers, like it or not. Finally I took her willingness to just stand still as an offer, and I slipped the halter over her head. She made no move to help. I rubbed her forehead. Then her shoulders, belly, hips, and again her face. She twitched, and pulled away, showing no warmth whatsoever.

I led her into the cowboy's arena and turned her loose. It was a small arena, but too large for a real Monty Roberts kind of *Join-Up*. Still, I had to try. I wanted to see if I could break through the iciness. When I unsnapped the lead, she took off like I was the devil himself, galloping full stride around and around and around. For the most part, I was just stood there, doing nothing, mouth agape.

After several minutes, the cowboy asked again, "Do you want me to catch her?"

"No, it's okay," I mumbled, feeling like I was the one on trial, not Mariah.

And she continued to run. I made a couple of token tosses of the lead line, but they were quite unnecessary. She ran on for a good seven or eight minutes with no apparent intention of stopping. I was getting dizzy. Finally I quit circling with her, turned my back to the biggest part of the arena, dropped my shoulders, and just stared at the ground.

And on she ran. Around and around. I felt the cowboy's eyes on me, probably saying: *What kind of an idiot are you? Get a grip and catch the horse!*

I was running out of will. But Mariah wasn't running out of gas. I was ready to give up when quite suddenly she jolted to a halt. Just like that. Maybe ten or fifteen feet behind where I was standing. I just stood there, staring at the ground. After a moment or two, she took a few steps toward me, then a few more. Monty's advice notwithstanding, I was peeking.

She never did touch me, but she did get within a couple of feet and just stood there. Finally I turned to her, rubbed her forehead, and snapped on the lead rope. I wanted to feel pleased, but didn't. It was willingness without emotion. Her eyes were empty. Like an old prostitute. *I know the gig. Let's get on with it.*

The cowboy then climbed aboard to demonstrate Mariah's skills. I suspect he was on his best behavior. He didn't appear to be particularly hard on her, but I noticed that his spurs seemed about two feet long and he did use them. She performed cleanly.

Then it was my turn in the saddle. Mariah pretty much did whatever I asked, but all the while, her lips were pouty and her ears were at half mast. Neither fish nor fowl. Not really showing any attitude, good or bad. Simply not into it. Not caring, one way or another.

Kathleen was next, woman to woman.

That's when I walked back through the gate and propped myself on the fence-rail with the cowboy. And that's when he said, "I've seen some of that natural horse pucky on RFD-TV and I've gotta tell you, the way I look at it that horse out there is here for one reason. My pleasure. And I'm gonna make sure she damn well understands that."

I think she did. And, now, so did I.

Clinician Ray Hunt opens every clinic or symposium the same way. "I'm here for the horse," he says. "To help him get a better deal." He and his mentor, Tom Dorrance, were the first to promote looking at a relationship with the horse from the horse's viewpoint. Mariah's owner wasn't willing to do that. His question would likely be: *What's in it for me?* Rather than, *What's in it for the horse?*

Perspective is everything, I was discovering. And I wanted desperately to change the perspective of the old cowboy. But what did I know? I was a newbie. A novice. Why would the cowboy or anyone else listen? I felt so helpless.

It would get worse.

As Kathleen dismounted, I looked deeply into this horse's eyes. I rubbed her, and the closer I got, the more she would turn her head, or step away. I tried to get her to sniff my hand, or my nose. That's what horses do when they greet each other. Sniff noses. All six of ours now go straight for the nose when we approach. Blow a little, sniff a little. And we return the greeting. Much nicer than the way dogs greet each other.

I reached out one last time to rub Mariah on the face, and she pulled away. Just enough. I turned to leave and quite without warning she stretched out and nuzzled my hand. Well, maybe it was more of a bump than a nuzzle. But as I turned back to look at her, it became very clear to me that this cute little mare had received everything I had given, she just had no clue what to do with it. Trust had never been part of her experience with humans.

On the ride home, I asked Kathleen, "So… what did you think?"

"No," she said flatly.

The silence telegraphed my surprise.

It seems that during her ride Mariah had spooked a couple of times at the dogs barking on the far side of the arena. That, plus the lack of any kind of warmth, had done it for her. Her blink, her first impression, was *no.*

Two weeks before she had been right on the money. I was all wrapped up in a palomino because he was gorgeous, but I was overlooking at least forty-six short-comings.

"What don't you like?" I had queried.

"Why would you even ask?" she said. And she was right. It was the wrong horse for us.

Kathleen and I had a deal. We would buy no horse that we didn't agree on.

But Mariah was different. I had finally seen a tiny light in the window. Until later I would have no idea how much she had been saying with that one little bump of my hand. How much of a call it was to take her away. Away from the cowboy.

I told Kathleen about the smidgen of connection, trying to open her mind, but it was locked tight. I felt depressed. I was certain this little mare, given the choice of Join-Up, along with time and good treatment, would come around. She would begin to understand what trust was all about. But I dropped the subject and it was very quiet on the long road home.

The next morning as we sat with our cappuccino looking out over the horse stalls, I brought up the subject again The next morning as well. And the next. I was haunted by that vacant look in Mariah's eyes, and the little bump of my hand. A cry for help. Which I believe to this day it was, but probably not as passionate a plea as I was portraying to Kathleen.

Finally, I'm sure just to shut me up, Kathleen said, "If you really feel that strongly about her, go ahead and get her."

She arrived the next day.

I was excited and anxious to get started, confident that the sincerity of my desire and my extensive working knowledge of the Join-Up concept – approaching a full month now – would win this cute little mare over immediately. I took her straight to the round pen.

No deal.

It didn't work.

She ran around and around, just as she had done the day we met. But no signals of any kind were forthcoming. After several minutes, she clearly wanted to stop, but she had not given me an ear. No licking and chewing. Nothing. So I kept her moving, wondering what I might be doing wrong. Perhaps she didn't know the language of the herd. Maybe she had never known a herd.

Doesn't matter, I objected. She's a horse, with fifty-five million years of genetics. It's in there somewhere. Has to be. I was beginning to reel with dizziness as Mariah continued to run circles around me. Finally, I gave up, put her in a stall, and retreated to the house to watch Monty's Join-Up DVD again.

I watched it twice.

If I was making a mistake, I couldn't find it.

Maybe Kathleen had been right. Maybe we shouldn't have purchased her.

Maybe she'd had so much bad treatment that she simply couldn't respond to anything else.

Think persistence, I kept telling myself, remembering the story of an Aborigine tribe in Australia who boasted of a perfect record when it came to rainmaking. They never failed to make rain. When asked how they managed to accomplish such a feat, the king simply smiled and said, "We just don't quit until it rains."

Back to the round pen, and more circles.

Two days of circles! Still no rain. I was determined that she was going to figure this out. But I was also becoming more and more convinced that she might very well have never been exposed to a herd; perhaps one of those horses who had spent her entire life in a stall, with no need for her native language. No opportunity to communicate with horses, and no desire to communicate with people like our friend, the cowboy.

Finally, on the third day, there was a breakthrough. Something clicked. After eight or nine trips around the round pen, her inside ear turned and locked on me. Then came the licking and chewing. Soon her head dropped and she began to ease closer. I let her stop, turned my back, and lowered my shoulders. Nothing happened for several minutes and I was about to send her off again when suddenly she walked up to me and stood, nose to shoulder. No sniffing, like Cash had done. But at least she had touched me. Of her own choice. And now she was just standing, instinct in control, but with no apparent understanding as to why.

It was enough. I was grinning from ear to ear.

I turned and rubbed her forehead and this time she didn't pull away. As I walked across the pen, she followed, right off my shoulder, making every turn I made. I gave her a good rubbing all over. Belly, back, hindquarters, everywhere. And I blew in her nose, and sniffed. She didn't respond, but she didn't move away either. I could almost see the wheels turning. *Do I know this greeting? Why's he doing that? I don't hate it really, but I'm not sure what it means. It does seem familiar.*

Somewhere, deep down in her brain, her genetics were finally bubbling to the surface, freed at last from the perspective of the old cowboy.

The next morning when I went down to the stables to feed and muck, I realized for the first time how completely the Join-Up process had transformed Mariah. She was a different horse, waiting by her stall gate, head stretched toward me, and she didn't move until I came over and gave her a sniff and a rub. A scratch under her jaw at the bend of the neck was her favorite. It became ritual. Every morning. And I dared not ignore her or she would scold me with a soft whinny or a snort. And then pull away when I finally came over, just for a moment, to let me know I had been naughty.

The simple act of giving her the choice of whether or not to be with me, of viewing all of her issues from her perspective, not from mine, had changed everything.

The new Mariah is as affectionate as Cash, as willing and giving, as anxious to see us... and until Skeeter came along she was Kathleen's favorite.

I can't help but wonder what the old cowboy would think if he knew that Mariah had learned what it means to trust.

The above is a re-written excerpt from the best selling book The Soul of a Horse – Life Lessons from the Herd by Joe Camp, written prior to Joe and Kathleen's discovery that horses were not genetically designed to be in stalls.

4

TO CHANGE

Dr. Marty Becker says in his wonderful book *The Healing Power of Pets*, "We should recognize the bond for what it is – living proof of the powerful connectedness between mankind and the rest of the animal kingdom. And the element of this powerful relationship that has always impressed me the most was the importance of nurturing another creature."

I wonder if those who don't believe that you can bond with a horse, also dismiss Dr. Becker's statement about the importance of nurturing another creature.

Not long ago I was hauling my tripod and video camera down our very steep pasture, struggling a bit because of sore ribs, a remnant from my fall off a ladder. I was moaning to myself about it as I set up the camera to videotape herd movement. Five of our six horses would soon begin their meandering climb back up the steep grade toward where the camera was set up. Only Mariah had remained at the top.

After a moment, I heard her shuffling up behind me. She paused at my back, lip-nibbled my shirtsleeve, then the most amazing thing happened. She nudged her nose between my arm and my ribs and pressed her warm muzzle softly against my rib cage. Precisely where it was hurting. She didn't move for minutes, until I had to shift position to start taping. It was a moment I didn't want to end.

How did she know?

Moreover, why did she care?

This is the horse whose relationship with humans was a blank stare when we first met her.

This is the bond.

Cash and Mariah are both what I call mutt Arabs (un-papered). They hang out a lot together. Not always, but I would say that they spend more time near each other than with any other horse in the herd. But that's it. No hugging and kissing. Not even any swapped grooming that I've ever seen. Yet, when Mariah broke the ice last winter in our pond and fell in she managed to get out on her own and make it back to the front paddock of the barn. (see *The Soul of a Horse Blogged*). When I found her, Cash was next to her pressing his body into hers, clearly trying to give her needed warmth. I never before or since have seen them that close together. Cash was there when she needed him.

Just as Mariah was there when I needed her.

But we must not only savor those moments. We must understand them from the perspective of the horse. Not try to force our humanness on them.

Kathleen and I spend regular time in the pasture, without agenda, to foster this bond. And to learn about our horses. The relationship, generated originally with Join-Up, which gave the horses the choice of whether or not to be with us, continues to mature because of our time in the pasture. And we become better communicators. Everything about the relationship gets better.

Time in the saddle, in the arena, and on the trail are important. But I believe the most important time is in the pasture. Just hanging out. It has done wonders for us, and our horses.

It continually strengthens their trust, our bond, and our relationship.

It teaches us about the horse, his habits, his language, his individual personality, and his genetics. How to read and understand what makes him tick.

It strengthens our leadership, and the horse's respect.

It dispels fear, both ours and theirs.

And it breeds confidence.

None of that can be injected, like a flu shot. It doesn't come as a flash when we wake up one morning, no matter how much we wish that it would. And even though books and DVDs have certainly crammed us full of insight and knowledge, they cannot replace the benefits of experience that come with being there, doing it, absorbing, learning firsthand.

Mileage.

And proving to them, just as with other humans, that you will first speak their language before asking them to learn yours. That you will do something they feel is worthwhile, before asking them to believe that what you want is worthwhile. Back before Benji our television commercial production company had just been assigned a large package of commercials from an advertising agency in Dallas and the dangling hope was that this group of commercials would finally thrust our demo reel into the big leagues. The spots were well written, well-designed, expensive commercials using recognizable Hollywood faces and the entire package would've normally been taken to Los Angeles for production, except for one thing. At the time, a certain lighting technique was in vogue on both coasts utilizing heavy fog filters in front of the lens so that light sources would blossom and bloom like the halos around street lights in a London fog. Glowing windows were especially the rage, simply achieved by hanging several thicknesses of sheer, translucent curtains, then lighting heavily from the rear so that, with a fog filter on the lens, the windows actually seemed to incandesce. Art directors across the country were in love with this *look*, so this is the look we had on our reel. We had discussed the approach with Dallas' top cameraman and much to

our surprise, he balked at the idea of *lowering himself* to
do *New York* lighting. He would stick with Dallas lighting, thank you, whatever that was. No glowing windows for him.

I tried to explain that gaining the confidence of
others is not an automatic process. First, show them
that you can do what *they* think is good, then, maybe
they'll listen to what *you* think is good. But he wouldn't
budge. I finally had to advise him that we would make
other arrangements for our camera work. After he left,
my partner exploded like a water balloon. "You
shouldn't've let him walk out mad! There's nobody else
in town we can trust with a job this big!"

"Yes, there is," I said, leaning back in my chair and
propping my feet on the desk.

"Who?!" he yelped, pacing back and forth. "Just
who?!"

"You," I said.

The color drained from his face. Then an uncertain
smile crept across his lips.

"Yeah?"

"Yeah," I said.

I knew exactly how I wanted the lighting to look
and I knew we had the knowledge, ability and good
sense to be able to work it out. Overnight, Jim became
the best New York cameraman in Dallas, and our reel
finally began to resemble the quality and philosophy we
had been selling. And agencies we had only dreamed of

working with were calling and sending storyboards for bids.

Try it with your horses. Show them that you understand life from their end of the lead rope.

Spending time with the horses also reminds us to always be thinking ahead, questioning, anticipating what could happen or go wrong by doing things this way or that.

Our time in the pasture, observing, studying, interacting at the horse's discretion, has taught us so much. That's why we wouldn't pay someone else to do the morning and evening feeding, even if our budget could afford it. Yes, there are mornings when we'd love to sleep in. But doing our own feeding guarantees no less than a couple of hours a day with our horses. Over time, those hours help to dissect and internalize each horse's individual personality, which determines how leadership is expressed in different ways to different horses. It provides insight into how weather affects their behavior. It has taught us, virtually by osmosis, how subtle our language can be, or not, with each unique horse. And it continually confirms us as members of the herd.

"I just never have enough time," one woman said to me.

"Then maybe you should acquire something that doesn't depend upon your leadership, relationship, compassion, and understanding for its health and happiness."

I didn't really say that, but I *thought* it. Under Kathleen's guidance I *am* learning :).

The bottom line is that when we put in the time and effort, when we got the relationship and leadership right, when we did it from the horse's end of the lead rope, not our own, our horses changed.

Every one of them.

Each differently perhaps, but change they did.

And always for the better.

Like Cash in the beginning, the others have never stopped trying, never stopped listening, never stopped giving.

And I promised him that day that he would have the best life I could possibly give him. And I meant it.

No stone would be left unturned because I now cared deeply about this horse and I would be asking everywhere I went how do I make his life better. Not how do I make *my* life better. My life would get better when his did.

And with that perspective it soon became very clear that there were things in his life that needed to get better. If what I was being told did not appear to be in the best interest of this horse who had trusted me and chosen me then I was not going to listen to someone else telling me what I needed to be doing to my horse that I loved and he didn't even know. I would get the answers myself. The true answers. Because I now had the passion to drive me through the barriers. And to withstand the onslaught from those who did not care about their horses as much as I did.

I rejected their lists. All those things you are supposed to do when you find yourself owning a horse. Or eight. And Kathleen and I set out to find the real answers for ourselves.

Now that we have eight horses living happy, healthy, stress free lives with none of the traditional problems and issues of so many horses living a more traditional life, what do you suppose has happened. Barely a day passes that someone doesn't tell us that what we're doing doesn't show up on their list of what one is supposed to do when one has acquired horses.

I can barely believe it.

But then Kathleen reminds me that we, too, were once there.

With our list.

Does anyone believe that Pat Parelli became one of the best horsemen on the planet by using a list? Or Monty Roberts? Or Ray Hunt?

That's why *The Soul of a Horse* and *Born Wild* are recommended reading. Because within those two books lies our entire journey to date and the passion shows through. If you don't have passion for what you're doing, for your horse, no list will make even the slightest difference in your success.

If you don't care enough about your horse to passionately want the very best life in the world for him or her, then none of what I've written before or here will make any difference whatsoever. To you or your horse.

**Watch the Video of Joe and Cash entitled
Relationship First!
The Soul of a Horse Channel on
Vimeo and YouTube**

Follow Joe & Kathleen's Journey
From no horses and no clue to stumbling through mistakes, fear, fascination and frustration on a collision course with the ultimate discovery that something was very wrong in the world of horses.

Read the National Best Seller
The Soul of a Horse
Life Lessons from the Herd

...and the #1 Amazon Bestseller...

Born Wild
The Journey Continues

Watch these videos on
The Soul of a Horse Channel on
Vimeo and YouTube:

How to Catch Your Horse in the Pasture

I Called Him… and He Came

Why The Soul of a Horse?

Born Wild
The Journey Continues

Miss Firestorm
Conceived in the Wild – Born to Us

Malachi
Our First Baby Conceived in the Wild

Benji Gets a New Baby… Horse

WHAT CRITICS ARE SAYING
ABOUT JOE CAMP

"Joe Camp is a master storyteller." *THE NEW YORK TIMES*

"Joe Camp is a gifted storyteller and the results are magical. Joe entertains, educates and empowers, baring his own soul while articulating keystone principles of a modern revolution in horsemanship." *RICK LAMB, AUTHOR AND TV/RADIO HOST "THE HORSE SHOW"*

"This book is fantastic. It has given me shivers, made me laugh and cry, and I just can't seem to put it down!" *CHERYL PANNIER, WHO RADIO AM 1040 DES MOINES*

"One cannot help but be touched by Camp's love and sympathy for animals and by his eloquence on the subject." *MICHAEL KORDA, THE WASHINGTON POST*

"Joe Camp is a natural when it comes to understanding how animals tick and a genius at telling us their story. His books are must-reads for those who love animals of any species." *MONTY ROBERTS, AUTHOR OF NEW YORK TIMES BEST-SELLER THE MAN WHO LISTENS TO HORSES*

"Camp has become something of a master at telling us what can be learned from animals, in this case specifically horses, without making us realize we have been educated, and, that is, perhaps, the mark of a real teacher. The tightly written, simply designed, and powerfully drawn chapters often read like short stories that flow from the heart." *JACK L. KENNEDY, THE JOPLIN INDEPENDENT*

"This book is absolutely fabulous! An amazing, amazing book. You're going to love it." *JANET PARSHALL'S AMERICA*

"Joe speaks a clear and simple truth that grabs hold of your heart." *YVONNE WELZ, EDITOR, THE HORSE'S HOOF MAGAZINE*

"I wish you could *hear* my excitement for Joe Camp's new book. It is unique, powerful, needed." *DR. MARTY BECKER, BEST-SELLING AUTHOR OF SEVERAL CHICKEN SOUP FOR THE SOUL BOOKS AND POPULAR VETERINARY CONTRIBUTOR TO ABC'S GOOD MORNING AMERICA*

Also by Joe Camp

The National Best Seller
The Soul of a Horse
Life Lessons from the Herd

The #1 Amazon Bestselling Sequel
Born Wild
The Journey Continues

#1 Amazon Bestseller
Horses & Stress
Eliminating the Root Cause of Most Health, Hoof & Behavior Problems

#1 Amazon Bestseller
Beginning Ground Work
Everything We've Learned About Relationship and Leadership

#1 Amazon Bestseller
Training with Treats
Transform Your Communication, Trust & Relationship

Why Our Horses Are Barefoot
*Everything We've Learned About the
Health and Happiness of the Hoof*

God Only Knows
Can You Trust Him with the Secret?

The Soul of a Horse Blogged
And Other Stories

Amazon Bestseller
Horses Were Born To Be On Grass
*How We Discovered the Simple But Undeniable
Truth About Grass, Sugar, Equine Diet & Lifestyle*

Horses Without Grass
*How We Kept Six Horses Moving and Eating Happily
Healthily on an Acre and a Half of Rocks and Dirt*

Dog On It
Everything You Need To Know About Life Is Right There At Your Feet

RESOURCES

There are, I'm certain, many programs and people who subscribe to these philosophies and are very good at what they do but are not listed in these resources. That's because we haven't experienced them, and we will only recommend to you programs that we believe, from our own personal experience, to be good for the horse and well worth the time and money.

Monty Roberts and Join up:
http://www.montyroberts.com- Please start here! Or at Monty's Equus Online University which is terrific and probably the best Equine learning value out there on the internet (Watch the Join-Up lesson and the Special Event lesson. Inspiring!). This is where you get the relationship right with your horse. Where you learn to give him the choice of whether or not to trust you. Where everything changes when he does. Please, do this. Learn Monty's Join-Up method, either from his Online University, his books, or DVDs. Watching his *Join-Up* DVD was probably our single most pivotal experience in our very short journey with horses. Even if you've owned your horse forever, go back to the beginning and execute a Join Up with your horse or horses. You'll find that when you unconditionally offer choice to your horse and he chooses you, everything changes.

You become a member of the herd, and your horse's leader, and with that goes responsibility on his part as well as yours. Even if you don't own horses, it is absolutely fascinating to watch Monty put a saddle and a rider on a completely unbroken horse in less than thirty minutes (unedited!). We've also watched and used Monty's *Dually Training Halter* DVD and his *Load-Up trailering* DVD. And we loved his books: *The Man Who Listens to Horses, The Horses in My Life, From My Hands to Yours, and Shy Boy.* Monty is a very impressive man who cares a great deal for horses.

http://www.imagineahorse.com- This is Allen Pogue and Suzanne De Laurentis' site. I cannot recommend strongly enough that everyone who leaves this eBook Nugget ready to take the next step with treats and vocabulary should visit this site and start collecting Allen's DVDs (he also sells big red circus balls). Because of his liberty work with multiple horses Allen has sort of been cast as a trick trainer, but he's so much more than that. It's all about relationship and foundation. We are dumbfounded by how Allen's horses treat him and try for him. His work with newborn foals and young horses is so logical and powerful that you should study it even if you never intend to own a horse. Allen says, "With my young horses, by the time they are three years old they are so mentally mature that saddling and riding is absolutely undramatic." He has taken Dr. Robert M.

Miller's book *Imprint Training of the Newborn Foal* to a new and exponential level.

Frederick Pignon
https://www.youtube.com/watch?v=w1YO3j-Zh3g
This man is amazing and has taken relationship and bond with his horses to an astounding new level. Visit the link above above and watch the video of his show with three beautiful black Lusitano stallions, all at liberty. This show would border on the miraculous if they were all geldings, but they're not. They're stallions. Most of us will never achieve the level of bond Frederick has achieved with his horses but it's inspiring to know that it's possible, and to see what the horse-human relationship is capable of becoming. Frederick believes in true partnership with his horses, he believes in making every training session fun not work, he encourages the horses to offer their ideas, and he uses treats. When Kathleen read his book *Gallop to Freedom* her response to me was simply, "Can we just move in with them?"

Natural Horsemanship: This is the current buzz word for those who train horses or teach humans the training of horses without any use of fear, cruelty, threats, aggression, or pain. The philosophy is growing like wildfire, and why shouldn't it? If you can accomplish everything you could ever hope for with your horse and still have a terrific relationship with him or her, and be respected as a leader, not feared as a dominant predator, why wouldn't you? As with any broadly based general philosophy, there are many differing schools of thought on what is important and what isn't, what works well and what doesn't. Which of these works best for you, I believe, depends a great deal on how you learn, and how much reinforcement and structure you need. In our beginnings, we more or less shuffled together Monty Roberts (above) and the next two whose websites are listed below, favoring one source for this and another for that. But beginning with Monty's Join-Up. Often, this gave us an opportunity to see how different programs handle the same topic, which enriches insight. But, ultimately, they all end up at the same place: When you have a good relationship with your horse that began with choice, when you are respected as your horse's leader, when you truly care for your horse, then, before too long, you will be able to figure out for yourself the best communication to evoke any particular objective. These programs, as written, or taped on DVD, merely give you a structured format to follow that will take you to that goal.

http://www.parelli.com- Pat and Linda Parelli have turned their teaching methods into a fully accredited college curriculum. We have four of their home DVD courses: *Level 1, Level 2, Level 3,* and *Liberty & Horse Behavior.* We recommend them all, but especially the first three. Often, they do run on, dragging out points much longer than perhaps necessary, but we've found, particularly in the early days, that knowledge gained through such saturation always bubbles up to present itself at the most opportune moments. In other words, it's good. Soak it up. It'll pay dividends later. Linda is a good instructor, especially in the first three programs, and Pat is one of the most amazing horsemen I've ever seen. His antics are inspirational for me. Not that I will ever duplicate any of them, but knowing that it's possible is very affirming. And watching him with a newborn foal is just fantastic. The difficulty for us with *Liberty & Horse Behavior* (besides its price) is on disk 5 whereon Linda consumes almost three hours to load an inconsistent horse into a trailer. Her belief is that the horse should *not* be *made* to do anything, he should *discover* it on his own. I believe there's another option. As Monty Roberts teaches, there is a big difference between *making* a horse do something and *leading* him through it, showing him that it's okay, that his trust in you is valid. Once you have joined up with him, and he trusts you, he is willing to take chances for you because of that trust, so long as you don't abuse the trust. On Monty's trailer-loading DVD Monty takes about one-tenth the time, and the horse (who was impossible to load before Monty) winds up loading himself from thirty feet away, happily, even playfully. And his trust in Monty has progressed as well, because he reached beyond his comfort zone and learned it was okay. His trust was confirmed. One thing the Parelli program stresses, in a way, is a followup to Monty Roberts' Join-Up: you should spend a lot of time just hanging out with your horse. In the stall, in the pasture, wherever. Quality time, so to speak. No agenda, just hanging out. Very much a relationship enhancer. And don't ever stomp straight over to your horse and slap on a halter. Wait. Let your horse come to you. It's that choice thing again, and Monty or Pat and Linda Parelli can teach you how it works.

http://www.chrislombard.com/ - An amazing horseman and wonderful teacher. His DVD *Beginning with the Horse* puts relationship, leadership and trust into simple easy-to-understand terms.

http://www.robertmmiller.com - Dr. Robert M. Miller is an equine veterinarian and world renowned speaker and author on horse behavior and natural horsemanship. I think his name comes up more often in these circles than anyone else's. His first book, *Imprint Training of the Newborn Foal* is now a bible of the horse world. He's not really a trainer, per se, but a phenomenal resource on horse behavior. He will show you the route to "the bond." You must visit his website.

Taking Your Horse Barefoot: Taking your horses barefoot involves more than just pulling shoes. The new breed of natural hoof care practitioners have studied and rely completely on what they call the wild horse trim, which replicates the trim that horses give to themselves in the wild through natural wear. The more the domesticated horse is out and about, moving constantly, the less trimming he or she will need. The more stall-bound the horse, the more trimming will be needed in order to keep the hooves healthy and in shape. Every horse is a candidate to live as nature intended. The object is to maintain their hooves as if they were in the wild, and that requires some study. Not a lot, but definitely some. I now consider myself capable of keeping my horses' hooves in shape. I don't do their regular trim, but I do perform interim touch-ups. The myth that domesticated horses *must* wear shoes has been proven to be pure hogwash. The fact that shoes degenerate the health of the hoof and the entire horse has not only been proven, but is also recognized even by those who nail shoes on horses. Successful high performance barefootedness with the wild horse trim can be accomplished for virtually every horse on the planet, and the process has even been proven to be a healing procedure for horses with laminitis and founder. On this subject, I beg you not to wait. Dive into the material below and give your horse a longer, healthier, happier life.

http://www.hoofrehab.com/– This is Pete Ramey's website. If you read only one book on this entire subject, read Pete's *Making Natural Hoof Care Work for You.* Or better yet, get his DVD series *Under the Horse,* which is fourteen-plus hours of terrific research, trimming, and information. He is my hero! He has had so much experience with making horses better. He cares so much about every horse that he helps. And all of this comes out in his writing and DVD series. If you've ever doubted the fact that horses do not need metal shoes and are in fact better off without them, please go to Pete's website. He will convince you otherwise. Then use his teachings to guide your horses' venture into barefootedness. He is never afraid or embarrassed to change his opinion on something as he learns more from his experiences. Pete's writings have also appeared in *Horse & Rider* and are on his website. He has taken all of Clinton Anderson's horses barefoot.

The following are other websites that contain good information regarding the barefoot subject:

http://www.TheHorsesHoof.com– this website and magazine of Yvonne and James Welz is devoted entirely to barefoot horses around the world and is surely the single largest resource for owners, trimmers, case histories, and virtually everything you would ever want to know about barefoot horses. With years and years of barefoot experience, Yvonne is an amazing resource. She can compare intelligently this method vs that and help you to understand all there is to know. And James is a super barefoot trimmer.

https://www.facebook.com/eddie.drabek
This is the website of Eddie Drabek, another one of my heroes. Eddie is a wonderful trimmer in Houston, Texas, and an articulate and inspirational educator and spokesman for getting metal shoes off horses. Read everything he has written, including the pieces on all the horses whose lives he has saved by taking them barefoot.

Our current hoof specialist in Tennessee is Mark Taylor who works in Tennessee, Arkansas, Alabama, and Mississippi 662-224-4158 http://www.natural-hoof.com/index.html

http://www.aanhcp.net- This is the website for the American Association of Natural Hoof Care Practioners.

Also see: Video of Joe: Why Are Our Horses Barefoot?

Natural Boarding: Once your horses are barefoot, please begin to figure out how to keep them out around the clock, day and night, moving constantly, or at least having that option. It's really not as difficult as you might imagine, even if you only have access to a small piece of property. Every step your horse takes makes his hooves and his body healthier, his immune system better. And it really is not that difficult or expensive to figure it out. Much cheaper than barns and stalls.

Paddock Paradise: A Guide to Natural Horse Boarding This book by Jaime Jackson begins with a study of horses in the wild, then describes many plans for getting your horses out 24/7, in replication of the wild. The designs are all very specific, but by reading the entire book you begin to deduce what's really important and what's not so important, and why. We didn't follow any of his plans, but we have one pasture that's probably an acre and a half and two much smaller ones (photos on our website www.thesoulofahorse.com). All of them function very well when combined with random food placement. They keep our horses on the move, as they would be in the wild. The big one is very inexpensively electrically-fenced. *Paddock Paradise* is available, as are all of Jaime's books, at http://www.paddockparadise.com/

Also see: **Video on YouTube: The Soul of a Horse Paddock Paradise: What We Did, How We Did It, and Why**

New resources are regularly updated on Kathleen's and my: **www.theSoulofaHorse.com** or our blog http://thesoulofahorse.com/blog See our entire menu under Bare Feet

The following videos are found on YouTube on The Soul of a Horse Channel:

Video of Joe: Why Are Our Horses Barefoot?

Video of Joe: Why Our Horses Eat from the Ground

Video: Finding The Soul of a Horse

Video of Joe and Cash: Relationship First!

Video: The Soul of a Horse Paddock Paradise: What We Did, How We Did It, and Why

Don't Ask for Patience – God Will Give You a Horse

Video: Shod Hoof
Video: Barefoot Hoof

Find a recommended trimmer in your area. There are links to the below on our website:

The American Association of Natural Horse Care Practioners

The American Hoof Association

Pacific Hoof Care Practitioners

Liberated Horsemanship Practitioners

Valuable Links on Diet and Nutrition:

Dr. Juliette Getty's website:
http://gettyequinenutrition.biz/

Dr. Getty's favorite feed/forage testing facility:
Equi-Analytical Labs:
http://www.equi-analytical.com

For more about pretty much anything in this book
please visit one of these websites:

www.thesoulofahorse.com

http://thesoulofahorse.com/blog

The Soul of a Horse Fan Page on Facebook

The Soul of a Horse Channel
on Vimeo or YouTube

Joe and The Soul of a Horse on Twitter
@Joe_Camp

Made in the USA
Lexington, KY
06 February 2018